SPOTLIGHT ON SPECIAL EDUCATIONAL NEEDS: SPEECH AND LANGUAGE DIFFICULTIES

Contents

Acknowledgement

The authors and publishers gratefully acknowledge permission given by Messrs Routledge to publish Extract Six on page 130 of *Versions of Primary Education* (1995) by Robin Alexander.

SPOTLIGHT ON SPECIAL EDUCATIONAL NEEDS: SPEECH AND LANGUAGE DIFFICULTIES

Introduction

For the majority of children of school age, speaking and listening are closely linked. Their language can be used in the teaching and learning of the curriculum and their communication skills can be further developed through curriculum and other activities. Most children, by the time they enter school, have well-developed grammar, a large vocabulary and are almost completely intelligible. However, there are some children whose understanding, or production of word or phrase structure, is immature or considerably different or undeveloped by comparison with their peers in similar contexts. Their ability to use language is limited and they do not seem to have the flexibility to adapt their language to the range of situations required in school and social life.

This book is concerned with children and young people who have particular needs in learning language and communication. Because they have not developed expected skills in speech and language, their teaching and learning are consequently affected. Their needs and difficulties appear in many different forms and are experienced for a variety of reasons. Although many of the children can be described as having 'specific' needs, with no other apparent difficulties in their development, some may have other associated difficulties such as hearing problems, physical difficulties or autistic spectrum difficulties. Increasingly, it is recognised that difficult behaviour may be linked with communication needs.

The book results from a collaborative writing activity between a teacher, a psychologist and a speech and language therapist. There are a number of ways of looking at language and communication needs and we recommend collaborative approaches because different views can be brought together and provide a broader perspective. Different professions will have their own ways of looking at problems. None of their approaches gives a complete explanation and they should be seen as complementary. In the field of language and communication, teachers, psychologists and speech and language therapists will often be expected to collaborate. Some understanding of each others' perspectives will be important for effective team work.

Ways of Looking at Language and Communication Needs

The terms 'speech and language difficulty', 'specific language impairment' or even the term 'language disorder', which is sometimes used, give no indication of *educational* need. The features of every child's language will be different and factors such as mother tongue, social background, experience and the influence of local linguistic variation will be important. We would prefer to talk about 'language and communication needs' as this suggests something that does not sit only within a child, but can be addressed and often met by those in the child's social and educational environment.

It is common to hear the terms 'delay' and 'disorder' in discussions of children's language but the distinction is often unclear. Some children use sounds, structures or words that would be expected from a much younger child. As they develop, their spoken language catches up and it is possible to say, in retrospect, that their language was 'delayed'. For other children, observation over time does not show this type of development. The structures of sounds and words are different from the patterns usually found in development. Their difficulties may be more long-lasting and are sometimes called language 'disorder'. However, it is usually only by following a child's development over time and in different settings that the nature of the needs can be described. It is also more valuable to describe a child's language skills in some detail than to arrive at a label which will have different meanings for different people.

While taking into consideration the wide variety of developmental patterns, children described as having language and communication needs do not learn language quickly enough to benefit from education that is accessible to the majority of their peers or in a way that enables them to respond to educational expectations.

Problems of imprecise definition make it very difficult to say, with real confidence, how many children have these needs. It is important to take notice of all children who appear to have difficulties in their early years so numbers will be greatest in the pre-school stages. Many children who appear to have difficulties when they begin school then develop communication skills quite rapidly, some with and some without help, and do not go on to have special educational needs. There are other children whose difficulties seem to become more prominent, or do not go away, as the demands of formal schooling increase. What is always noted is that about twice as many boys as girls experience these difficulties, although this observation has not yet been satisfactorily explained.

O the book 6

Difficulties can be observed in any aspects of language and the effects on communication will be different in every case. The child's language may be characterised by a range of features which may include aspects of comprehension, expression or both. Intelligibility may be affected by the omission, substitution, distortion or sequencing of sounds or by features of stress, intonation or voice quality. A difficulty can occur at different levels: grammar, meaning or the function of language. Expression may be limited or may comprise long sentences that are empty of meaning. Some pupils, however difficult they are to understand, will appear quite uninhibited and talk incessantly, while others may say very little although they are responsive to other people. Because written language is based on spoken language, many children with speech and language needs also have problems with literacy. The analysis of literacy skills introduced by the National Literacy Strategy can be helpful. Children at all stages are expected to work at word, sentence and text level and these can be used to specify a child's strengths and needs.

Some approaches look in detail at the language of an individual pupil, but it is also important to consider overall communication in the context of life in the classroom, at home or in other social settings. Before deciding that a child has a speech or a language difficulty it is necessary to look at different circumstances in which communication takes place. The communication skills of the adults who live and work with the child will be important in reducing or increasing the effectiveness of the child's communication efforts.

Educational and Social Approaches

The classroom

In school, language is the main vehicle for providing information, asking questions, making demands and for the social relationships on which all of these activities are based. One of the first tasks for the investigation of a suspected language difficulty is to examine the language of the classroom. In research in primary classrooms, it was noted that:

'children were offered few opportunities to talk in a structured way, and most of the relatively small amount of oral work which took place involved talking by the teacher and listening by the pupils'.

(Alexander, 1995, p.156)

7

Analysis of adult language is therefore an important element in making decisions about whether a language difficulty exists or not. We should ask whether the teacher's language can be reasonably understood by the pupils in the class and whether each pupil is given similar opportunities to talk. Curriculum areas have their own particular sets of language: the use of 'times' in maths and 'time' in history can be confusing; 'seconds' on the clock are different from 'second' in a line. There are thousands of examples of potential confusion every day in classrooms. One of the most useful activities teachers can undertake is to tape record themselves talking in class and then to analyse the recording, either alone or with a colleague. It is useful to ask questions such as: Who spoke most, the teacher or pupils? How long were the pauses after the teacher stopped speaking? Were they long enough to give pupils time to respond? Were there any incomplete sentences, or changes of idea in the middle of a sentence? If the teacher seems to be talking too much, too quickly or unclearly, then this may suggest why some children seem to have 'language difficulty'. A teacher was heard asking the class to 'put your hand up if you're a school dinner'. While most people understand what was meant this may not really give a chance to the child who processes language more slowly than others.

Analysis of the language of the curriculum is the other important task in identifying language needs. New or potentially tricky vocabulary must be identified before planning the tasks for teaching and learning for a range of pupils in any class. After following a scheme of work, the teacher will need to find ways of ensuring that every individual has understood, and can use, all of the new ideas.

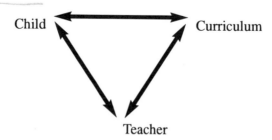

Figure 1: The interaction of language in school.

Language in school therefore is usually a combination of the language required for the curriculum and the language used by teachers and pupils. Adaptation and explanation of language are important if a range of pupil needs are to be met.

At home

Inevitably, parents and professionals see children differently. Language and communication are different at home and at school in the same way that different behaviour is acceptable in different settings. It is important not to confuse language style with language difficulty. Information about language and communication will be needed from a child's home and it is essential that parents or other family members are included in providing details about communication skills. They will need to say, for example, whether they believe there is a speech or a language problem and if so, how different members of the family experience it. Parents will know how their children are similar and different and will be able to say whether any of their children talk more or less competently than their siblings or their friends in similar circumstances. A helpful structure for exploring a child's communication skills with parents, or indeed with anyone who knows the child well, is the *Pragmatics Profile of Everyday Communication Skills in Children* (Dewart & Summers, 1995). This interview schedule explores communication in a range of settings for a variety of purposes. It can help to form a picture of opportunities for communication and how a child and other important people respond to the opportunities.

Examination of language at home and in school provides a social or educational view of language and possible explanation of language difficulty. It can suggest some changes to behaviour or overall planning which may help pupils who are thought to have particular language needs. Modification of language is an important element in differentiating activities in school for all pupils.

Approaches That Consider Linguistic Behaviour

In the discussion above, we suggested some questions to be asked about teachers' language. These questions focus on the way in which language is being used and may form the beginnings of more detailed linguistic analysis. Examples of spoken language in different circumstances can be analysed in terms of the structure of the language, the meaning of the language and the ways in which the language is being used. Linguistic analysis, sometimes called 'language profiling', is often among the tasks undertaken by speech and language therapists in deciding on the nature of a language difficulty. Teachers and therapists will need to work closely together at this stage to ensure that the language analysed comes from a range of activities typical for the particular child.

Analysis of a language sample can provide an enormous amount of information. Firstly, if the utterances are taken from a conversation between two people, close examination may suggest that one is not understanding the other. Further analysis may suggest that this is because one of the conversational partners does not speak clearly or does not appear to 'make sense'. If the partners are a child and an adult, the adult may seem to make sense, but the child may appear not to understand, and either not reply, or respond with an irrelevant utterance.

Speech may be 'unclear' in many ways. The sounds of the words may not be made in the conventional way and the difficulty may be described either as 'phonetic' or 'phonological'. Phonetic problems are usually in the production of sounds, the intonation of utterances or in the stress or volume of what is said. Phonological problems are in the sound patterns which distinguish the meaning of spoken language. For example, a child may be unable to make sounds at the back of the mouth and so replaces all 'back' sounds with 'front' sounds. Words such as 'car', 'key', 'cart', 'good' and 'sky' become 'tar', 'tee', 'tart', 'dood' and 'sty'. The meaning of what is said may therefore be ambiguous.

Apparent problems with sounds, however, may not be so simple. Difficulties in producing the sounds at the ends of words may affect grammatical structure. A person may not be able to convey plurals if they are unable to make 's' or 'z' sounds; they may not be able to say something in the past tense if they are unable to produce 'ed' at the ends of verbs. All of this will inevitably affect the meaning of what they try to say and will probably mean that their language lacks the flexibility needed for expression in different circumstances. One level of language is usually interlinked with another.

Linguistic analysis can be undertaken in a progressively detailed way and can be helpful in pinpointing a specific level or aspect of language.

Curriculum documents can be helpful in focusing on difficulty at a particular level of language. For example, in England, the curriculum for English Attainment Target 1 focuses on speaking and listening. Examples of skills in speaking and listening emphasise pupils' ability to:

'listen to others and usually respond appropriately' (Level 1);
'speak clearly and use a growing vocabulary' (Level 2);
'begin to adapt what they say to the needs of the listener, varying the use of vocabulary and the level of detail' (Level 3);
'… use appropriately some of the features of standard English vocabulary and grammar' (Level 4);
'… they pay close attention to what others say, ask questions to develop ideas and make contributions to take account of other's views' (Level 5);

'their talk engages the listener through the variety of its vocabulary and expression.' (Level 6)

(DfEE & QCA, 1999)

Curriculum documents describe language in terms of clear fluent speech, organising what is said, choosing words with precision, taking account of the needs of the listener, conversational conventions, such as turn-taking, asking questions, use of verb tenses, expanding vocabulary. By taking examples of language in the classroom, it is possible to see whether a child seems to have particular difficulty with any of these aspects of language and therefore whether there seem to be problems with the content or meaning of language, the structure in the grammar or the sounds, or in the use of language for different purposes with a variety of people. There is a great deal of potential here for discussions between teachers and speech and language therapists.

Medical and Biological Approaches

Traditionally, people interested in speech and language difficulties or indeed many other types of learning difficulty have attempted to find reasons for the problems. If a cause can be found, then a 'cure', or at least some treatment, might be suggested. This approach is sometimes referred to as a 'medical model' or way of thinking. Many medical or physical problems can indeed by thought about in this way. Infection leads to illness and today many illnesses are cured by medication; surgery too may be extremely effective in alleviating distress. Some speech and language problems may partly be approached in this way. A hearing problem, in a teacher or a pupil, may lead to communication difficulties. Hearing must always be investigated if speech is unclear. This approach will also be necessary to look into breathing difficulties, movement problems, structural problems or neurological disease. In some cases, medical intervention will make an essential contribution to appropriate management.

The medical approach may play a particular part when speech and language therapists and teachers try to collaborate. Therapists are usually employed by the health service and have traditionally worked in clinics. Schools provide a different setting with a different vocabulary when talking about children and their needs. An important task for teachers and therapists who work together will be to make sure that they understand the specific terms each of them uses.

11

Psycholinguistic and Cognitive Approaches

The fourth approach to language and learning difficulties, which is becoming increasingly useful, is a focus on how a person is learning. In the case of language, this means looking at how the child processes language, that is, what seems to be going on underneath what we can see and hear the child saying and doing. The approach is developing from information in cognitive psychology, neurology and linguistics which suggests ways in which the brain processes information. It is sometimes referred to as a cognitive-neuro-psychological approach. Educational psychologists may use it to develop a cognitive profile of an individual; speech and language therapists may call it psycholinguistic profiling because of the particular focus on language skills.

Using this approach to language will lead us to ask a child to undertake a number of tasks. These will attempt to look at aspects of memory, visual processing, auditory skills and the coordination of movement. They will analyse how a child is taking in information and how they are encoding or expressing it. For example, two children may seem to have similar difficulties with language in the classroom. Their spoken language may appear almost the same. Investigation may suggest that one of them has problems in the organisation of movement which affects the production of sounds; the other does not produce clear speech because the analysis of sounds, or auditory input, is inaccurate and so sound production is affected. These children will need different approaches to therapy and teaching.

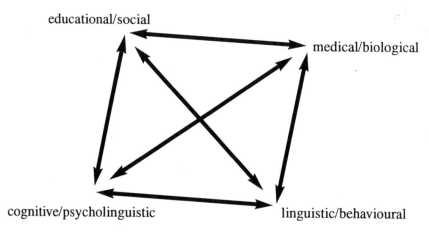

Figure 2: The combination of approaches to speech and language difficulties.

As we said earlier, there is no single approach to la
communication needs but each of the approaches above ha
contribution to make. Each will take on a different emph
individual case. A combination of approaches which links
knowledge and skills of parents and professionals offers m
success than work in isolation. The key to the successful combination of
approaches is effective communication between all concerned.

Particular Difficulties: A Brief Overview

Speech and language difficulties occur in many different forms and some
may not be immediately apparent. For this reason, children with language
learning needs can be misconstrued. They may be accused of difficult
behaviour if they show frustration at not being understood; they may appear
not to listen if they have difficulty in following spoken language. They are
often considered 'slow' or are labelled as having other learning difficulties
if they do not speak clearly or cannot find the right word. It is important to
note that almost all of the features found in the language of people with
'difficulties' are found in 'normal' speakers and in the speech of children
whose development gives no cause for concern. However, children who are
described as having specific speech and language difficulties, disorders, delay
or needs show these behaviours more frequently and in a range of contexts.

Attention and Listening Difficulties

We need to pay attention to something before we can take in information
from it and understand it. Listening involves further development of auditory
attention. Most people are selective in their attention. They attend to what
is salient or interesting to them to the extent that it is possible to fail to
hear or see what else is going on. Adults and children who have achieved
appropriate levels of attention for learning in school can usually switch
their attention from one thing to another and back again. Although children
are sometimes described as having a long (or good) attention 'span', this
does not really tell us much as attention is more complex than a simple
quantity. The length of time we attend to something relates very much to
its interest level for us. Some children may have difficulties in paying
attention, particularly to linguistic information, and this will inevitably
relate to difficulties in learning to understand language. These children

, be easily distractible and seem more interested in sounds and activities outside the room than what is being said directly to them. They may be more interested in visual than auditory activities and they may not be very skillful at controlling their own attention. They may therefore miss sounds, words or large chunks of language so that they do not grasp the whole meaning. Spoken instructions that contain too much information at once may therefore cause great difficulty. They may challenge and frustrate their teachers and they may be singled out for having difficult behaviour.

Detailed observation of children over time will need to note the quality of their attention in terms of what they are most interested in and the conditions under which they pay attention.

It is rarely enough simply to identify a child as a poor listener. All of the following can lead to poor listening on the part of the child:

- hearing loss;

- a poor memory for speech sounds, words or phrases;

- emotional insecurity and anxiety. Look for other evidence of this;

- difficulties with the comprehension of language;

- difficulties with pragmatics, especially in relation to identifying topics and following changes in topic.

Understanding

Attention is the first step to understanding but there are children who hear, pay attention and listen, yet still have difficulties in understanding language. This may be at the level of the meaning of words, which are fundamental to our understanding of the world. For example, some words will signify aspects of size, shape, colour, position or time. If these terms are not understood there may be serious implications for the child's functioning in the classroom and across all areas of the curriculum. There may also be difficulties at more complex levels where words are linked together. Understanding may be affected by poor memory skills which will interfere with the ability to remember individual elements of language or to remember sounds or words in the correct sequence. Children whose speech and language difficulties are characterised mainly by problems of comprehension are also likely to show problems in expressive speech.

14

Expression

Difficulties with sounds

A child may understand what is said but have their main difficulty in the expression of ideas. For example, some children will have a very limited repertoire of sounds in their speech. They may, for example, 'favour' a particular group of sounds, such as those made with the tip of the tongue behind the top teeth – 't' and 'd'.

Sentences such as the following may be heard:

Dayi do mi a dayi a di me   (try to say this aloud)

The person who cracks the code here will see that 'g' and 'k' sounds are substituted by 'd' and that other sounds are omitted. They understand that the child has said 'Daddy got me a garage at Christmas'. Sometimes the cracking of the code, that is understanding which sounds are substituted for others, often quite consistently, is all that is necessary to understand the child and prevent extreme frustration. Other children are less consistent in their production and may have difficulties coordinating the fine oral movements required for speech. They may need alternative ways of expressing themselves, such as by illustrations or by using a signing system.

Difficulties with grammar

The production of sounds in spoken language is also related to the expression of grammatical meaning. The meaning of words changes with the use of 'morphemes', the small units of grammar that carry meaning; 'ed' and 'ing' on the end of a verb will indicate past or future tense; 's' may denote plural or possession. A child who has difficulty with the production of sounds may not be able to express grammatical differences and it will be important to determine whether this difficulty is, in fact, due to a problem with sounds or difficulty with grammatical understanding.

For these children, collaboration between teachers and speech and language therapists is essential. Therapists will usually analyse the child's speech production in detail and suggest how to approach their unintelligible utterances.

Difficulties with words

Some children may have specific difficulties in learning the meanings of words. Words have a symbolic function; some are linked in a very direct way with objects or activities; others, for example 'if', 'and', 'how', 'where', are less concrete. Words are learnt in context, through use and association with ideas both concrete and abstract. Although apparent difficulty with words for some children may relate to lack of experience, others may have difficulty in learning words because of specific difficulties with association of linked ideas or with memory.

In addition to their meaning, words, like sounds, also have grammatical functions. They can function as nouns, pronouns, adjectives, verbs, adverbs, prepositions, conjunctions and interjections. Many words function differently in different contexts. For example:

a) She's writing a letter.

b) The writing is on the wall.

c) I must get a new writing pad.

In a) 'writing' serves as a verb; in b) it is a noun; in c) it acts as an adjective. Children who have difficulties in developing word meaning will experience difficulties in expressing grammatical differences.

Social Use of Language

The difficulties described above mainly relate to the meaning and the structure of language. They are clearly linked. However, there are some children and indeed adults too who appear to speak quite well but seem to have difficulties in using language in social settings. Detailed observation of their utterances and the settings in which they occur suggest that they have difficulties in saying what is appropriate to the occasion and to their conversational partner(s). This is not simply social ineptness, although that is one of the results of the difficulty. For these children, language does not always function for them in a useful way. The difficulties may be apparent in the topic of conversation and the ability to maintain the topic. They may seem unable to take account of other speakers by responding to their questions and comments. Children with these so-called 'pragmatic' difficulties may appear bizarre or rude and they may gain a reputation for poor behaviour. Linguistic pragmatics, or language use, is strongly linked with language meaning or semantic aspects. While in theory it is possible to make a distinction between pragmatics and comprehension, in practice it is more difficult because pragmatic problems arise from a failure to understand how language is used, rather than to what it refers. The children are sometimes described as having semantic and pragmatic difficulties but this is another label that needs a great deal of 'unpicking'. Examination and analysis of the child's language in a wide range of situations will be essential to identify the specific features of the problem. Collaboration between teachers, parents and speech and language therapists can be critical in these cases. Before deciding that a child has a behaviour problem, shown by non-compliance or negative behaviour, it is always worth checking their ability to use language appropriately for different purposes.

Language as an Overlapping and Integrated System

From the descriptions above it is evident that language and communication are not always what they appear on the surface to be. A difficulty that affects speech sounds can result in problems with grammatical structures, which will also affect the ability to express meaning. A child who has difficulties in learning the meaning of words may not be able to use appropriate expressions and may appear socially 'odd'. Detailed linguistic description can be one way to determine where the difficulties lie. A useful first stage in this process is to try to identify whether the child's difficulties in expressing or understanding language seem to be predominantly in the content, the form or the use of language. This approach to the development of children's language and to the analysis of difficulties was proposed by Bloom and Lahey (1978). As children's language develops, aspects of content, form and use come together and overlap as in the diagram shown below.

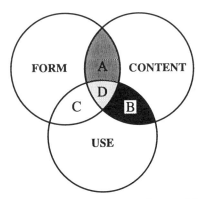

Figure 3: The interaction of content, form and use of language (Bloom & Lahey, 1978).

Content refers to the ideas and concepts of language, described as the *semantic* or *meaning level* by linguists.

Form is the structure of language represented by sounds in spoken language, by symbols or letters in written language, and by gestures and signs in signed language. Each of these forms of language will have morphemes and words. Form relates to the *syntactic* or *grammatical level* described by linguists.

Use of language is its function, that is how it is used for a variety of purposes with different audiences. This is what linguists call the *pragmatic level* of language.

Managing Speech and Language Difficulties

The *Special Educational Needs Code of Practice* envisages that the needs of the child will be exposed by the difficulties that they are experiencing in the classroom (Department for Education and Skills, 2001). It describes how these difficulties should be explored and how attempts to support and teach the child should be pursued. The starting point for identifying children is, then, the classroom. Below we describe different areas of developmental difficulty and how they may appear in the classroom in our target group of children. We then take each of these areas of difficulty and explore the way in which they can be highlighted by classroom observation and linked to support and teaching strategies designed to address the children's special educational needs. We have extracted some of the key questions to ask oneself during observations. They form an Observation Guide in Appendix 1 at the end of the book.

We have taken a scenario from Robin Alexander's research into primary school practice in Leeds (Alexander, 1995). This research was interested in the overwhelming organisational complexity to which children were subjected within the classroom. In the following scenario, in which we consider the language of the teacher, the work of the afternoon is being explained to a primary school class. The children have been divided into four groups and the teacher has drawn them together to listen to his instructions.

Read through this transcript and try to grasp the main ideas the teacher attempts to put over. Try to identify the specific demands being made on the pupils through language.

18

1	Mr I:	First thing: people in the green group, if you remembered to bring your library book back, go to your drawer and get it now, and go to the library with Ms X. Everybody else sit very quietly *(waits for the children with library books to leave)*.
5		K come and sit near L.
		Now, people who are left, sit up nicely and look at me.
		I'm going to let another group this afternoon try some of the collage pictures of the birds this afternoon. The yellow group did some really nice pictures this morning;
10		if they're not quite finished you'll be able to finish them tomorrow.
		The first group who are going to try the collage this afternoon is the blue group.
		Yellow group this afternoon are going to start with some
15		tens and units sums.
		The red group are going to finish off those cards we were doing this morning, and then we're going to do some more writing about the different kinds of clothes that we're wearing ... that we can wear.
20		If you're working in the wet area, the blue group, you've to be sensible. You've to be careful with the glue and the scissors. Don't stick one big piece of material for the whole shape of the bird: cut the material into small pieces and put different material to make up a pattern for the body
25		of the bird. That way it looks much better when it's finished. I want to see the yellow table working each one on your own to begin with this afternoon, not doing the sum with your friend or the person sitting next to you, but doing it
30		on your own, to see what answer you're going to get ...
		Red group: when you've finished the card that you were doing from this morning, then you draw the picture that's on the white sheet and leave enough space to put the words that go with the different pieces of clothing, and I will come
35		and read them to you.
		So; if the blue group go quietly outside there are some pieces of paper with the shape of a bird already on them, and there are some blank pieces.
		...
	Mr I:	...

40 Mr I: Red table go and sit down.
            M, the green table went to the library.
    M: I forgot my book.
    Mr I: You forgot your book? You look at a book in the book corner
            while your group comes back. You look at a book in the book
45   corner while your group comes back. Yellow group come and
            sit down ...

(Alexander, 1995, p.130)

As the children move away to begin work, there is one child who appears to have little or no idea of what is required. This may be indicated by any or all of the following behaviours:

1. A failure to carry out tasks as requested.

2. A tendency towards 'disobeying' instructions or requests.

3. A tendency to join activities after they have begun because he is relying on copying other children.

4. A noticeable preference for looking around at others rather than listening.

5. Getting the 'wrong end of the stick' in conversations and saying odd things.

6. Inexplicably falling out with other children.

If we return to the teacher's instructions it will be possible to discover a number of areas in which the child could have found particular difficulty.

Difficulties with social use of language
Let us imagine that the child belongs to the yellow group and that he or she has a difficulty with the use of language for different purposes. This is known as a 'pragmatic problem' and would manifest itself here in difficulties in responding to communication appropriately. The first occasion on which the child will need personally to make sense of the teacher's instructions will be in relation to the activity of making collage pictures in which he or she has taken part in the morning. From lines 6 to 11 the teacher's utterances constitute the kind of 'social warm-up' that would be familiar to most teachers in most classrooms, drawing the children together, gaining their

attention, delivering a broad statement about the afternoon's activities and adding some words of praise. It would be seen as good social practice by most teachers. However, for a child with difficulties with the social use of language, it may present real problems. Such children may fail to process whole utterances or to select relevant information. They would therefore latch on to parts of the teacher's instructions and fail to select the pertinent details, that is, 'topic clues' which are, in this case, that if the work is not finished they will be able to complete it the next day.

The key issue here is that the topic of a conversation or the point of an activity is more fundamental than language and actions themselves. - Children have a developing ability to imagine themselves in 'other people's shoes' and it is this ability that is constantly at work in all of us, to maintain the vital sharing arrangements involved in conversations and activities. Imaginative projection is required in order to grasp the topic of conversation and to appreciate the changes and shifts that are likely to occur afterwards. Children with pragmatic difficulties have weakness in this ability. Their comprehension can break down when topics are not well marked or are changed frequently and when changes are poorly signalled. Teaching strategies would therefore need to minimise topic change, explain very clearly what is going on and take greater care to establish the topic. Sometimes it can be helpful to say 'we are talking about x'.

Even more difficulty awaits our child in the later part of the teacher's instructions. In lines 27 to 30 it can be seen that the information concerning maths refers only to the manner in which the 'sums' are to be carried out; not to the actual work itself. Our child will have to have retained the information already given briefly, that the yellow group would be doing sums that afternoon. The child with pragmatic difficulties, like any child with language learning needs, may well also have very poor attention skills and be highly distractible. They may therefore have entirely missed the early reference. Alternatively, they may fail to put the two pieces of information together to enable them to make sense of the message but, more likely still, will be unable to interpret the language that is relevant to their particular situation and thus make use of what they need to know.

A further potential area of difficulty is highlighted by the word 'remembered' in the first sentence. 'Remember' is a word that refers to a mental state or a concept of mind. Other examples of this type of word are 'think', 'forget', 'feel', 'wish', 'consider', 'hope', 'worry'. They refer to a reflective understanding of language, known at a more technical level as 'meta-language'. They may be problematic words for some children, in particular, those with pragmatic problems.

In the scenario the term 'remembered' would hold particular difficulties for our child if, indeed, he or she was in the green group and was the child named 'M'. The teacher's form of address would again expose a difficulty with imaginative situations, which require well-developed 'sharing arrangements' in order to make inferences. The teacher tells M that the green table went to the library but there is an implied question 'what are you doing here?' Thus he is making a statement which implies his question and M has to infer what the question is. Discerning implied meaning is a developing ability and it can be a sensitive comprehension area for a wide range of children; indeed, adults sometimes misread implied meanings. A common example occurs when somebody comes back unexpectedly and the person they have just left says, 'Have you forgotten something?' The person returning could simply reply 'no' but the questioner really means 'Why have you returned?'

Observation of pragmatic difficulties

The general comprehension skills of children with pragmatic difficulties can be investigated informally by spending some time in a one-to-one or group situation and in the course of the activity checking whether the child is able to process whole utterances and select pertinent details.

Children with pragmatic difficulties often have particular problems with inference so it is possible to take a simple story such as:

'Patsy got on the train to go shopping in London. She sat down. The ticket collector came along and Patsy realised that she had dropped her purse with the ticket and money in so she had to get off at the next station.'

Then ask:

'How did Patsy travel to go shopping?'
'Who came up to Patsy?'
'Why did Patsy have to get off the train?'
'Did Patsy go shopping in London?'

Note particularly that children with pragmatic difficulties often show particular problems with the understanding of question words, for example 'who', 'what' and 'how'.

Another simple informal observation can be achieved with a semi-structured conversation. This is best done with picture material so that the adult can retain a certain amount of control in the situation. Make a note of:

22

- the child's turn-taking skills;

- topic maintenance, that is does the child frequently change the topic of conversation or introduce new topics with scant regard for the needs of the listener?

- Does the child signal the need for clarification if he or she does not understand what is being said and, conversely, does the child clarify what is meant if the listener signals a lack of understanding?

- Does the child ask relevant questions?

- Is what the child is saying appropriate?

It is worth noting here that many children show some difficulties in these areas at some times but the child you are concerned with will be showing atypical patterns of language most of the time.

Consider the child at play. Are the child's chosen activities age-appropriate and imaginative? Is the child slow to learn the rules of group games? Does humour tend towards the visual and slapstick? Is there poor appreciation of jokes and plays on words?

Difficulties in all these areas may point to a problem with the social use of language (pragmatics) and it will be useful to request further investigation by a speech and language therapist. Further information and practical suggestions about these difficulties can be found in *Teaching Talking*, a screening and intervention programme for children with speech and language difficulties by Ann Locke and Maggie Beech (1991) and in the book *Inclusion for Children with Speech and Language Impairments* by Kate Ripley, Jenny Barrett and Pam Fleming (2001). The *Pragmatics Profile of Everyday Communication Skills in Children* (Dewart & Summers, 1995), mentioned earlier (page 9) in our discussion of parents' views, is also an excellent assessment tool.

Classroom support for pragmatic difficulties

There are a number of ways in which children with pragmatic difficulties can be helped in the classroom setting. Such activities may be included in daily routines and need not require extra time or extensive planning.

Activities involving making inferences
- Using story books and reading scheme material. The Oxford Reading Tree (1986) is useful for this purpose since it has an established group of characters with particular personalities which afford scope for prediction. Children can be helped to make inferences from pictures, particularly the 'punch line' of the story, which is characteristic of the Oxford Reading Tree. Very often children with pragmatic problems are excellent at reading accuracy but fail to comprehend what they are reading. They can be helped by encouraging them to read and then asking them questions about the text.

- Guessing games: for example, hiding an object behind a screen. The child has to guess what it is from clues. A variation is for the members of the group to choose to be an animal and give clues to the others to guess their identity: for example, 'I have long ears and whiskers and a fluffy tail...'

- Games, home-made or published such as 'Guess Who' where one child has to ask appropriate questions of a partner in order to eliminate pictures that do not match a chosen item.

- Deduction games may be helpful using picture material and games in which one child has to give explicit instructions to another to carry out a particular task. Play group guessing games, in which one child gives clues to the others about an object, animal or character, which the group then have to guess.

Activities involving issues of shared knowledge and provision of sufficient information
- Identify insufficient information: Give an instruction with no reference, for example, 'put it back'. Discuss why this command is unclear and then gradually build up the information:
    'put the ruler back'
    'put it back on the table'
    'put the ruler back on the table'

- Activities in which children have to place items on an outline drawing according to instructions from a partner, for example, placing windows, doors, chimney in position on a house.

- Games in which children have to make telephone calls to each other for a particular purpose.

- Appropriate behaviour in a social context. Adults act out a situation, for example, between 'customer' and 'shop assistant' or 'pupil' and teacher'. Discuss appropriate verbal and non-verbal behaviour. Children then take turns.

Consideration of causal relationships

- Imaginative small-toy play: for example, use of the Playmobile to show a road accident. Ask, 'Why is the ambulance coming?' Alternatively this could be done using picture material.

- Answering 'why?' questions from a story. Picture-sequenced stories are particularly useful for this.

- Made or bought games that have a 'track' to follow. The child has to explain the inferential meaning of the picture when they land on a particular square.

Non-verbal abilities

- Use pictures to discuss, interpret and model facial expressions.

- Miming games: for example, actions, people, animals, emotions.

- Discuss possible responses of people in pictorial material: for example, how someone might be feeling if being chased by a large dog.

- Match picture cards to spoken description: for example, 'he is very tired'.

- Becoming aware of 'personal space': for example, two children gradually approach each other until one or both says, 'stop'. Then check that this is a distance at which they feel comfortable for talking. See if it is the same for other pairs of children.

- Try having a conversation back-to-back or where children cannot see each other. Discuss the outcomes.

Turn-taking activities

- All games and activities that involve turn-taking can be useful. Additionally many daily classroom routines provide opportunities for practising this skill.

- Children sit in a circle and roll a ball to a named person. Adding the requirement that the 'sender' and the 'receiver' have to make eye contact before the ball is rolled is a useful extension to this game.

- 'Pass the ...' games.

- 'Whispers' in which a whispered message is sent around the circle with the last person saying the message out loud.

Awareness of self in a group

- Games in which the child has to make a contribution while remembering the contributions of others: for example, 'I went to market...'

- Simon Says.

- Games involving 10–20 questions where children have to avoid asking the same question twice.

- Games involving the use of questioning to establish the identity of features of a particular item: for example, children have to establish the attributes of a two-dimensional shape which has been removed from a collection of shapes – 'big, yellow, triangle'.

Conversation skills

Initiating a conversation

- Role playing what to say in particular social settings.

- With older children, record conversations on video and discuss successful and unsuccessful ways of beginning conversations.

Maintaining the conversation

- In small groups, work on: how to ask questions; how to follow the topic of another child; appropriate signalling when the child wants to join the conversation.

- Adults model a conversation which 'goes wrong': for example, poor listening, speaking too quickly (see also the suggestions on shared knowledge above). Discuss what went wrong.

- Following the activity above, discussion can focus on how to ask for clarification.

Difficulties with Comprehension

Difficulties with comprehension often remain undetected at home where conversations are supported by familiar routines and the tapestry of family life. If we now return to our classroom scenario we can see what might happen to a child who has difficulty understanding language.

If the child belonged to the green group, he or she might be alerted to the need to listen by the teacher's opening line. However, the very word 'first' raises issues. Words for ordinal positions are relatively late vocabulary acquisitions for children and the teacher's phrase 'first thing' might just be heard as 'social noise' by a child with comprehension difficulties. Further potential pitfalls are ahead. An important message is conveyed by the small word 'if' in line 1. It is a conditional. A failure to understand the role of the word 'if' in this instruction would have implications for everything that follows and could easily lead to children without a library book going out with Ms X. The child in possession of a library book becomes part of a group who are then subject to further instructions. In this 'treasure hunt' situation our child has to process, understand and act on each clue as it arises if they are to become and remain part of the group who are on their way to the library.

As the teacher gathers the group to him, his language, as noted, becomes a mixture of an attention-gaining device, a sketch of the afternoon's activities and some words of encouragement. Encompassed within this are two important pieces of information, the first being that the yellow group's unfinished collage can be completed on the following day and that the next group to tackle the task will be the blue group. Here, children with comprehension difficulties would have to cope with another 'if' which might or might not place them in a group completing a collage. A child would also have to cope with several shifts of topic as the teacher comments on work to be undertaken, praise for work in progress, when work can be completed and which group will be next. In this situation our child has to make sense of a mixture of relevant and irrelevant information and act upon it, separating off largely irrelevant social language and extracting key instructions that will dictate the afternoon's activities.

Social and referential language

When the teacher uses a phrase such as 'sit up nicely and look at me' or 'the yellow group did nice pictures', he is using a different form of communication from when he gives detailed instructions. It is helpful, in a classroom, to think of two types of language. The first type we will call 'social language'. It refers to language such as 'good girl, Melanie' or 'sit up nicely'. The second type we will call 'referential language' or 'knowledge language'. Language, as we have already noted, is first learnt as a means of social contact. Its use as a structured system for recording human knowledge comes later and is a great deal to do with schooling. Teachers slip easily between the two types of language but in developmental terms, it must be remembered that children have to move gradually from the first to the second. Children with language difficulties may have mastered social language but be struggling a long way behind peers with vocabulary knowledge. The easiest place to see the process happening is in the language of maths and science. The social use of a term such as 'more' extends to the notion of more food, for example 'more beans'. However, when a teacher refers to 'more beans', it is likely to be not a splodge on a spoon but as a number of beans. Teachers will recognise these issues around many terms such as 'middle', 'every', 'least', 'equal', 'pair' and 'fewest', as well as ordinal terms such as 'first' which is mentioned in our scenario. Teachers need to be conscious of when they make precise references and to recognise this use as a potential area of difficulty for children with language difficulties.

A useful tool for gaining an estimate of children's referential or knowledge vocabulary is the Boehm Test of Basic Concepts (Boehm, 1986). It uses pictures to test children's understanding of key concepts such as 'first', 'top', 'few', 'middle', 'between', 'alike', both alone and in combination, for example, 'Mark *every* box that has a ball at the *centre.*'

If we turn now to the blue group we can see a further set of difficulties for a child with a comprehension problem. The blue group instruction that begins 'if you're working in the wet area' uses instructional language that is out of sequence with the required sequence of the activity. The actual sequence is:

1. Stated objective – make up a pattern for the body of the bird.

2. Scissors (object).

3. Different material (object).

4. Cut material into small pieces (action).

5. Glue (object).

6. Stick (action).

However, the order of mention is:

- Glue (5).

- Scissors (2).

- Stick (6).

- Cut material into small pieces (4).

- Different material (3).

- Stated objective: make up a pattern for the body of the bird (1).

Where the order of mention is different from the activity sequence, language comprehension is taxed. The most common instances of this difficulty come with the use of the passive voice; an example (not in the transcript) would be 'the cakes will be shared by the children' and also in the use of the time (temporal) markers 'before' and 'after', as, for example, in 'before you get your Unifix cubes out, put your rulers away'. A teacher could help children's understanding by ensuring that their language parallels the action – 'put your rulers away then get your Unifix cubes out'.

It is important to note that we are not attempting to discourage complex language. Where appropriate, children's skills need extending and they need to experience this kind of language. We are concerned rather to point out where complex language could present difficulties for a child with speech and language difficulties. If such a child is being addressed, then differentiation based upon the observations noted will be needed. All of the suggestions made rely on adults being aware of their own language and how it influences the child's understanding.

If we move on now to the red group there is another area of potential difficulty for the child with language comprehension difficulties. In our extract, the group is given an instruction to 'draw the picture that's on the white sheet and leave enough space to put in the words'. This message contains detailed reference to material and has to be comprehended exactly and carefully. It calls for practical judgement, that is, 'seeing' the page in one's mind's eye, which is implicit and needs to be inferred. A child with a comprehension difficulty would be much helped if the teacher held up the white sheet and showed the children the spaces for the picture and words. For the child with a language comprehension problem, demonstration relieves the language load by paralleling verbal information with visual information. It is a vital differentiation strategy.

Observing comprehension

Children with comprehension difficulties may have problems with question words. They may not be able to follow instructions without prompting. They may give unexpected responses to questions and have difficulty with words that change their reference in different circumstances, for example, 'sister', 'mother', 'brother'. They may make literal interpretations of colloquial phrases such as 'pull your socks up'. Also, because of the tendency to interpret language literally, they may have particular difficulty with metaphors and similes and with humour, jokes and sarcasm. If you listen to the child you may be able to collect evidence of comprehension difficulties at the level of vocabulary, grammar and organisation of ideas. It is also possible to gather information informally which will assist the speech and language therapist in subsequent investigations and illuminate the child's strengths and weaknesses for the purposes of day-to-day management.

Look for a difficulty in apparently making sense of whole sentences and give some thought to how these are being processed by the child, for example, in the following exchange:

T. 'Those are nice socks, Robyn.'
R. 'Yes, I'm at 5 to 8.'

Robyn had picked up the word 'socks' and made an ambiguous statement about their size. Spending some time considering responses like this can throw light on a child's problem quite clearly even in the early stages of investigation.

30

Also, consider whether the child in school at Years 2, 3 and beyond is able to listen attentively to stories told over a period of time; is the child able to remember details and discuss various aspects and key issues? Does the child ask questions to promote his or her own understanding?

In considering the best approach for the child with comprehension difficulties there are several points to remember about classroom language. The child with speech or language needs may not be fully conversant with the social meanings of language before moving on to more precise meanings. For example:

Social meaning	Referential (knowledge) meanings
more/no more	one more
more beans	a few more
	more/less
	50 more

In the context of social meaning, the opposite of 'more' is 'no more'. Although beans are countable when I ask for more beans, I do not expect the server to ask 'how many more' I want but 'how much more?' In the context of knowledge meaning, the opposite of 'more' is 'less' and it is a countable concept.

This is not just about vocabulary or words in combination but by following grammatical rules new meanings are constructed. For example, failure to understand the future conditional tense might lead a child to misconstrue the sentence 'James would have jumped the fence but he saw the puddle just in time.'

Strategies to assist comprehension

The monitoring of teachers' own language is the most vital principle in work with children with speech and language needs. It is important for teachers to be aware of their own language and to find extra strategies for supporting children with comprehension difficulties. Such strategies could include:

- Simplify sentences.

- Reword sentences.

- Repeat key sentences and ask the child to repeat back what they have to do.

- Keep the order-of-mention the same as the order-of-action.

- Interweave directions and actions so that large chunks of language do not need to be understood and remembered.

- Mark clearly when attentive listening is required. Selectively name children with poor listening attention.

- Identify topics clearly, minimise topic changes and signal these changes before they happen.

- Work specifically on the vocabulary that is required. Do not assume understanding of basic concepts. Be alert to one's use of precise referential or knowledge terms. Check the child's understanding of key referential terms such as 'middle'.

- Use more literal language for those children who have difficulties with social language use and meaning.

- Be alert to one's use of idioms such as:
  Cut it out
  I was just pulling your leg
  Have you got ants in your pants
  Help Melanie out, William
  By all means use these, but it may be necessary to check that children have understood them and, if not, explain what they mean.

- Break up the presentation of verbal messages, repeat them and ask the children to repeat them.

- Make rules and expectations logical, chronologically ordered and explicit.

- Within the curriculum success may depend upon whether children are told or shown. Always demonstrate and show whenever possible.

When children are working in collaboration with others, facilitation from an adult may be needed to ensure that the child with comprehension difficulties is not marginalised. These children will need:

- support to understand and use the words with which to influence the behaviour of others in situations that involve turn-taking, sharing, attention-getting from adults and peers;

- help in learning how to negotiate;

- support for listening skills and responding appropriately to what others say;

- help, explicit instruction and visual demonstration of the rules of games;

- help in talking with the teacher. This is an opportunity for the teacher to use language that is 'mapped' on to the comprehension level of the child. Use all supplementary cues available, for example showing, gesture, mime, signing. Obtain evidence that the child has understood by encouraging non-verbal communication if necessary.

Comprehension problems can be difficult to track down. If it is suspected that a child has difficulties with comprehension or if the teacher finds themselves adapting to a child in any of the ways described above then a referral to a speech and language therapist should be made. The teacher's observations, with specific examples from the conversations in the classroom between children and between adults and a child, will make a vital contribution to assessment and to records of progress.

Language and Memory Difficulties

If we return to our classroom scenario, it will be possible to detect another potential area of confusion for the child with speech and language difficulties. If we revisit the blue group, patiently waiting to begin their bird collage, a further difficulty will become apparent; quite simply, they are having to remember what has been said to them. Clearly, this kind of time lapse between instructions may be problematic for many children, but there are also more subtle hazards for a child with a particular language processing difficulty. Many children with speech and language difficulties have a poor memory for what is said and for them speech sounds 'disappear' before they can understand them. When following an instruction the language has to be remembered until the actions have been completed. For example, the green group will have had to be able to retain and act upon three pieces of information, namely 'go to your drawer, get it (book), go to the library'. Had the teacher been aware of the presence of a child with a language difficulty, he could have asked the green group to go and get their library books and then have sent them to the library. This would have removed the complex language and replaced it with a simple sentence followed by an action, followed, on completion, by another simple sentence, followed by another action.

There are many ways in which teachers can detect memory difficulties in an informal way. For example, can the child retain rote learning, for example, days of the week, months of the year, number bonds? Can the child recite rhymes and remember the words of poems and songs? Does the child have difficulty in retelling events in chronological order? Do they have difficulty in ordering a sequence of activities that are required to complete a task? Does the child have difficulty in remembering three or more items in short-term memory or have a poor long-term memory for single words?

Where children have difficulties in remembering, it is helpful to simplify language and to reduce the memory load by breaking up instructions into manageable 'chunks'. Children can also be asked to repeat back what they have been asked to do either in their own words or in the form in which the directions were given. Simple cartoon drawings or little symbols sequenced from left to right or from top to bottom on a piece of card or paper can be very helpful as a mnemonic. Clearly, the sequence of drawings needs to be in the correct action-order. For children with adequate reading skills, a list of key words can also support a poor verbal memory. In our example a drawing or key word list would be something like this:

Figure 4: Key word list with symbols for action.

Attention Difficulties

Finally, in addition to the particular language difficulties that have been revealed by our classroom observation, the child may also have a poor ability to maintain attention. When the children are sent away to get on with their given tasks, our child may well be seen to be having difficulties with concentrating on the task.

In the extract there are a number of examples where clear signals are not given about which group the messages are for and thus difficulties are created for the child who has poorly developed attention skills. For example, the collage pictures are referred to well before the message is given that the blue group will be doing them. Two other groups of children are given messages before the blue group is addressed again. They are initially addressed without any alerting signal: 'If you're working in the wet area, the blue group'. Many children with speech and language difficulties have problems with attention and listening and require very clear alerting when a message is for them. In this case, identifying the group clearly and giving them all their instructions would help. In addition it may be necessary to first say their name to alert them.

Strategies for development of attention skills

There are a number of ways in which teachers can assist a child to develop the skills of attention, listening and concentration. These include:

- Giving clear signals when it is necessary to listen carefully and indicating when the message is for someone else.

- Allowing the child to work in a quiet area away from distraction.

- Giving the child some individual time to build up the experience of sustained attention.

- Choosing appropriate times to introduce tasks requiring sustained attention when the child is likely to be more receptive, for example, early in the day or week.

- Choosing appropriate activities which are interesting and motivating and keeping expectations simple.

Classroom Organisation

Before leaving this classroom scenario there are a number of general points which can be made about classroom organisation. While they are intended to help a child with difficulties of language, they will constitute good classroom practice for all pupils. These are:

- Be aware that the noise level may present difficulties for some children. Organise the classroom so that there are quiet places for children to work if they wish to do so.

- Try to avoid too much whole-class discussion. Consider organising more small group work and discussion.

- Try to set aside time to engage children in conversation, particularly those about whom you are concerned. Do not use closed questions such as, 'Are you enjoying this?' but try to get a feel of the child's current language competence by holding an extended conversation.

- Record findings briefly – a box file is a good idea for jottings about observations. Do not make it an onerous task. Little and often will build a picture surprisingly quickly.

We have so far looked extensively at what are termed 'receptive' language difficulties and what can happen to children in a classroom when, for a variety of reasons, they fail to understand the language of their learning environment. Many of the suggestions given show how children's difficulties may be reduced by modification of the language used in the classroom. We now turn to children who have difficulties in expressing themselves.

Difficulties with Expression

Some children will appear to understand all that is said but may seem unable or unwilling to speak. It is not advisable to describe a child as unwilling to communicate until the possibility of expressive speech and language difficulties has been investigated. The most obvious place to start is a talk with the parents about the child's communication at home and whether or not they have ever been referred to a speech and language therapist. A child with expressive speech and language difficulties can easily be marginalised by the quick, 'jumping in' characteristic of young children's verbal communication. A teacher taking a group has to accommodate to this and the group is more easily managed if articulate children are used to move the action and topic on. As children get older the emphasis on social intercourse switches increasingly to verbal communication. Lack of intelligibility may become a severe problem for a child and can make successful social and emotional adjustment well nigh impossible by seven and eight. At this age, extensive social strategies as well as learning support systems may need to be linked with specialist speech and language therapy. In the classroom there are a range of measures that can assist children with expressive difficulties and, in some cases, the child can be encouraged to communicate through drawings, symbols, gesture and mime. This avenue leads, of course, in extreme cases, to the area of alternative communication with formal systems of sign or symbol such as Paget Gorman, Signed English, Makaton, Rebus and Blissymbolics.

Teachers will be increasingly concerned about non-participating children. Such children may appear to understand what is said and follow well the pattern of activities. However, they may be on the edge of the group, never commenting in class or group discussions and rarely initiating conversation. They may speak more when with one or two peers in play, or in unstructured time, but when the teacher speaks to the child the response is usually monosyllabic. The child may say only individual words or phrases and sounds are sometimes muddled. This type of expressive language difficulty may remain hidden as the child can be thought of as 'quiet'. However, they may speak little because of an underlying difficulty in organising the structure or meaning of language.

Other children with expressive language difficulties may also speak little by comparison with their peers. What they do say is often unintelligible. This type of expressive difficulty is due largely to the child's inability to produce the sounds of speech appropriately to convey meaning. The teacher cannot understand the child and struggles to find a context. Sometimes the child becomes irritated by the teacher's failure to understand. With classmates the child can be boisterous and physical. Commonly the child is in trouble for 'pushing' and 'fighting'. This can be understood as the child using physical means to convey a message or to ease frustration arising from their limited communication. If behaviour is a problem, it is worth checking whether spoken communication skills are developing satisfactorily.

Difficulties with expression and intelligibility may occur in different aspects of language. There are some children whose difficulties are manifested more in muddled phrases, clauses and sentences in addition to difficulty with accurate pronunciation. Some words may be 'telescoped' so that 'vegetables' is pronounced 'vegbles', 'elephants' becomes 'ephants'. Other words are distorted, such as 'peruter' for 'computer', 'potiter' for 'helicopter'. The boundaries between words may appear blurred as if the child does not appreciate that these are separate words. Such children may adapt by keeping their sentences short. There can often be a considerable gap between the child's actual understanding of spoken language and their ability to show that they understand it. These children often have disorganised actions as well and they can have problems in showing what they understand through what they make, draw or arrange. It is very common for these children to be judged as lacking in understanding and ability and care must be taken to ensure that comprehension and expression are investigated separately. These are often children who do better on some formal psychometric tests and they may become the subject of disagreements between educational psychologists and teachers. They may see the child's performance very differently and come to different conclusions about their level of 'intelligence'.

There is a range of reasons why a child may be reluctant or unable to communicate effectively verbally and the difficulties may be at the level of sounds, words or grammatical structures. These are:

- They may have a difficulty in thinking of the correct word or words to use (a word finding problem).

- They may not have an adequate vocabulary.

- They may not be able to put a sentence together.

- They may not be able to pronounce words.

- They may be self-conscious about their pronunciation.

- They may have such a poor verbal memory that they are unable to use it to organise what they are going to say.

A child may have a combination of any of these difficulties. Take note of their mistakes because these will provide an insight into the area or areas in which the difficulties lie.

Classroom strategies for expressive language difficulties

Children with such problems can be helped in a number of ways to organise their responses. These include:

- 'Modelling strategies'. When children produce utterances that are inadequate because they are incomplete, ungrammatical or difficult to understand, direct 'correction' is not usually advisable. However, in informal situations, for example if the child says something when going out to play, a correct version of the utterance can be spoken by the teacher, without comment and without requiring any imitation by the child. Special activities devised by the speech and language therapist can be helpful to address the development of a child's skill in this area.

- The creation of 'space' so that the child can talk. The teacher needs to 'suppress' other children and encourage, reward and make time for communication for the child who is struggling with an expressive language difficulty. The importance of this strategy cannot be overstated as a child with limited expression is inevitably marginalised within a classroom unless positive steps are taken.

- Children with expressive difficulties can engage in better communication when their idiosyncrasies are known. They cope better with adults and children who have learned their speech patterns. Emotional adjustment may be best secured through a small circle of friends and familiar adults. The placement of the child with the same small group of peers for all or part of each day may be recommended.

In addition, there is a range of ways of helping children with expressive speech and language difficulties through written language and through use of their often superior visual skills. The following strategies may be helpful:

- Encourage the child to use simple line drawn cartoon sequences or symbols as a support framework for writing an account or story. Alternatively, a key word list can be generated.

- When constructing sentences, ask the child to contribute key words. Provide the remaining words to generate the sentence. Write the words on pieces of card and ask the child to sort them into a sentence. The activity of sorting gives the teacher the opportunity to discuss the child's choice and order of words. Thus, the activity will make use of

39

known sight-vocabulary, for example, 'I', 'to', 'the', 'went', and will use initial letter clues, such as 'What does "swimming" start with?' Word-order skills will be developed grammatically in understanding and use.

- Word processing can be used to assist the strategies outlined above. The use of carefully selected written words that can be assembled, written out, arranged or typed on a computer can give the child a chance to work on new sentence types and to practise incorporating newly learned individual words or parts of speech.

Children with expressive language difficulties may be greatly helped through the development of their reading skills. An effective route can be taken by using material from a reading scheme with a controlled vocabulary which will be extended logically and progressively over what might be a protracted period of time. The acquisition of a sight vocabulary can be started very soon after school entry and together with phonological work on syllable division, onset and rime and phonemes, will provide a powerful tool for enhancing both written and spoken language skills.

On entry to school, the child with expressive language difficulties may often be thought, by the teacher, not to be ready to begin learning to read. Conversely, if the child does begin to learn, a teacher may feel there is little engagement with the text, and an inability to make use of context, appreciate a storyline or predict what might happen next in a story. By giving the child a sight vocabulary and decoding skills as early as possible, a framework is provided from which comprehension and language knowledge can be extended in terms of structure, meaning and use. If the child has access to print, a stable resource is then available which can provide a teaching tool for spoken language in its own right.

Many children who have had difficulties with speech and language in their early years go on to have significant problems with text comprehension at a later date, even when they have appeared to be reading at an age-appropriate level by seven to eight years old (Conti-Ramsden & Botting, 1999). Helpful strategies for these children might include modifying the text by summaries, mind maps, icons and diagrams; working on the text by highlighting or key-wording; focused discussion to promote the development of inference and prediction skills; and training in imagery which uses the visual system to support remembering. Again, the strategies that are used to support reading comprehension can also be helpful for children who have difficulties with processing spoken language.

Working with Older Pupils

So far we have given a picture that focuses sharply on the young primary-age child because it is at this stage that the widest range of needs are found. However, there will be pupils with speech and language difficulties throughout all the educational stages. As children enter late primary and secondary education, language limitations, rather than speech, become the major issue. By this stage there is a very strong link with written language. Many children with written language problems have a history of spoken language difficulties, although this may rarely be acknowledged as the pupil's spoken language may appear to be unproblematic. An older child with written language difficulties needs to have their history of spoken language problems re-examined. The following questions should be raised:

- In what areas did the child have difficulty?

- What residual problems did they have?

Limited grammatical ability, poor vocabulary and word-finding problems are common, yet unrecognised, language difficulties among older children. Children with pragmatic difficulties may continue their struggles with idioms and metaphor and may have problems with the language that refers to mental states: 'feel', 'pride', 'remember', 'reflect', 'embarrassment'. With all of these young people, the close working of spoken with written language is vital. After the age of five, written language is the major factor in the development of spoken language. This in itself points to the need for close working between teachers and speech and language therapists who will need to ensure that they are working on similar themes and skills. For different types of problem, written language is helpful in different simple ways.

Grammar
- In reading, sentences can usefully be separated into their core and 'add-in' words, that is, phrases and clauses. For example, 'The (red) box (on the dresser) was left open by the (scared) burglar.'

- In writing, children can be helped to expand their sentences by 'adding-in' words and phrases.

- Another strategy useable in both reading and writing is to help the child re-form the sentence in a different tense.

Vocabulary
- In reading, children can be questioned about word meanings or asked to give alternatives.

- In writing they can be asked to give alternatives or be given suggestions.

- Word-finding: Written words act as another representation of a word. This gives the child with a word-finding problem another route to a word, provided they can read the word. As with speech, the sounds of syllables, onsets, rimes and letters are vital. These are likely to need teaching through to sixth form level, as are prefixes and suffixes (*un*helpful; *un*tidy; helpful*ness;* tidy*ness*).

Pragmatic difficulties
In reading and writing, accompanying questioning and discussion is vital. The basic principle is to constantly question the pupil with pragmatic difficulties about their reading. Questioning can range over the following:

- Literal questions that can be answered directly from what the text states.

- Inferential questions that require the pupil to draw conclusions. These often take the form, 'How do we know that…?'

- Questions about the meanings of words.

- Questions about the behaviour, motives, interests and likely future actions of characters.

- Questions about the story structure and how events might unfold.

- Questions designed to tap the pupil's background knowledge.

The teacher's questions will reveal the pupil's understandings and misunderstandings and hence provide opportunities for instruction and development.
Older children with language difficulties can find secondary education verbally very demanding. Diagrams, pictures, drawings and models with a variety of print size, spacing and arrangement graphics are more common at primary than secondary levels. At secondary school, information and

instructions are often given verbally with little or no repeat and a minimum of time to record. Differentiation is bringing more visual presentation into secondary teaching but many pupils need to make extensive use of such methods.

In secondary subject-teaching, new vocabulary is introduced at a prolific rate. Knowledge terms, all used with strict reference, abound. In some subjects the sentences used to refer to the objects of interest are long, complex and full of 'add ins' as well as introducing new vocabulary. This is most true of science. Practical experiments and demonstrations are vital for pupils with language difficulties. Often, with a little effort the key ideas can be presented in simpler language or even described using metaphor; for example, water flow is often used to illustrate the flow of an electric current, including linking water volume to amps and water pressure to volts.

Teachers and Speech and Language Therapists

The *Special Educational Needs Code of Practice* makes particular reference to the provision of speech and language therapy and points out that:

'... since communication is so fundamental in learning and progression, addressing speech and language impairment should normally be recorded as educational provision (in a statement) unless there are exceptional reasons for not doing so'.

(8:49)

The message here is that a child's language and communication needs will be addressed within the educational setting as far as possible. If School Action (5:43) is considered necessary, the Special Educational Needs Coordinator (SENCo) will help in collecting information about a child and will assist in planning extra help from within the school. External services will be consulted if a child fails to make expected progress within the plan made by the school. In the case of children with language and communication needs, external services at the stage of School Action Plus (5:54) are likely to be provided in the form of speech and language therapy. Teachers and speech and language therapists will then be expected to work together to meet the child's needs as far as possible within school. While the majority of speech and language therapists are employed by the health service, a few may be employed by schools. Some are based in health centres, serving a large community including schools and nurseries. Although still not universal, an increasing number now offer a service to

43

mainstream schools where they work in classrooms and offer guidance to teachers and learning support assistants on children's needs.

The Code of Practice points out that schools, LEAs and the NHS should cooperate closely in meeting the needs of children with communication difficulties (8:51). Whatever arrangement is in operation, success can only be achieved by collaboration between teacher and therapist and a mutual understanding of each other's way of working. In order to achieve collaboration, teachers and therapists need to understand that there are differences in the way that they think about speech and language. Therapists and teachers are 'brought up' differently and trained during their initial professional education to think and work in different ways. If the difference is appreciated, the strengths of both can be utilised to their best advantage.

Some of these differences were illustrated earlier in this book when we presented ways of looking at speech and language. First, we suggested educational and social approaches. These will be familiar to teachers. We then described approaches that focus on linguistic behaviour; medical and biological considerations; psycholinguistic and cognitive aspects. These largely represent the ways in which speech and language therapists think about difficulties.

Educational and social approaches to language place emphasis upon the social process, that is, on the act of communication, which takes place in educational, social and other settings. Language is seen as the primary tool for learning and as the means by which ideas are transmitted between people. Other perspectives look at the nature of speech and the nature of language, which may be identified with linguistic, biological and cognitive aspects of language. This leads us to analyse the elements of speech and language and to examine what underpins them. Teachers then may be more concerned with children's attainment *when* speaking and listening. Speaking and listening are the tools by which learning and teaching are achieved. Speech and language therapists emphasise attainment *within* speech and language. They are interested in the achievement of speech and language in its own right. A combination of these views will be necessary where a child has communication difficulties in a classroom. It will be necessary to examine the components of language and how these appear within the teaching and learning in the classroom.

Questions that a teacher would ask might include:

- Is the child interested?

- Is it what they want to be doing at the moment?

44

- Do they know enough about what we are talking about?

- Are they tired, hungry, emotionally distressed or anxious?

- Have they experience of this situation?

- Are they concentrating, looking, listening?

They are questions that a modern teacher with a child-centred perspective would ask if a child's performance in speaking and listening was of concern.

The question that may not be asked is, 'Has the child the underlying skills to speak or listen?' It is always necessary to check whether children can do something before assuming that they are in some way being prevented from doing it.

Questions about the underlying skills and components of language might include:

- Does the child understand the sentences that I am using?

- Can the child find the vocabulary to express ideas?

- Can the child put together a sentence that clearly expresses meaning?

- Can the child articulate the words that he or she intends to speak?

Speech and language therapists are likely to ask questions of this nature but may be less focused on language in social contexts.

In considering these differences of approach it is important to remember that they interact with each other. Much of our skill with language and with our particular ways of talking develops within the varying situations in which we find ourselves. Teaching and learning promote the use of language in 'real' situations and we do not usually have to concern ourselves with how this is achieved. The need to communicate with others acts as a stimulus to promote speech and language skills. This is why it is important to deal with language and communication difficulties within the school setting as far as possible.

It is important for teachers to understand the nature of their own perspective as well as that of their therapist partner if they are to find ways of working that allow for the establishment of a flexible, negotiated approach. The purpose will be to incorporate the aims of therapy, which may target specific language skills, into the reality of daily activities in the classroom.

It is only by talking and sharing expertise and opinion that true collaboration can take place. This requires time and commitment. The rewards, however, are great for both teacher and therapist. Both increase their professional expertise and create a common body of knowledge and experience which will assist the teacher in classroom planning for all children. For the therapist, a knowledge of how classrooms are organised will allow for realistic planning. Increased knowledge of curriculum demands will facilitate precise and targeted programmes using, for example, topic work.

Research with teachers and therapists suggests that in order to work productively together, time is needed for discussion, planning and evaluation of their actions (Wright, 1996; Lacey, 2001). Time cannot be stolen from the classroom when other demands are on the teacher. Therapists and teachers should expect to have timetabled time together, without the pressure of classroom activities. In this way, time with pupils with speech and language difficulties can be spent productively. The implication here is that headteachers and SENCos will actively promote and endorse teachers taking legitimate time outside class time to talk to therapists.

Individual Educational Plans (IEPs)

The speech and language therapist's advice will need to inform the IEP. Although the IEP contains individual teaching targets, details of teaching methods, staffing and resources and pupil groupings, it is vital that it is written for the classroom context. If classroom experience is not taken into account, the plan could focus excessively on the individual and might propose activities to add into an already busy curriculum and social system. It is essential to assess the classroom and curriculum for the special learning opportunities they present. Unless this is done, real learning opportunities will be missed. It is particularly important for the special educational needs coordinator and speech and language therapist to work on the most helpful marriage of literacy and spoken language for the pupil. When this stage of classroom opportunities and support has been exhausted, then and only then should small-group and finally individual teaching time, activities and materials be specified.

When drawing up Individual Education Plans for children with speech and language difficulties, consider the following:

- Language is a means of thinking about, and responding to, the world.

- Language is a powerful tool for learning.

- Language is a fundamental means by which learning contexts are created and developed by teachers.

- Children's communication skills are enhanced and developed through the curriculum and other activities.

The IEP should therefore reflect an approach that addresses the language issues that are embedded in the classroom perspective and that manifest themselves in teaching style and the creation and organisation of learning contexts. It should also incorporate enhancement of the particular speech and language competencies that have been highlighted by speech and language therapy assessment.

There are particular issues that need to be taken into account when constructing an IEP for a child with speech and language difficulties. We have outlined these points below, taking the headings from the Code of Practice 'Strands of Action to meet SEN'.

1. Assessment and planning

When considering the nature and level of difficulty the following are important considerations:

1. the fundamental linguistic difficulties as they present to the speech and language therapist. These may be complex in nature but it is important for teachers to acquire an understanding of them if they are to adequately describe and address:

2. the difficulties as they present within the curriculum, for example the effect of phonological difficulties on the acquisition of reading skills or the effect of difficulties with linguistic concepts such as 'except', 'either/or' or 'instead of' on the development of notions of cause and effect and the ability to predict;

3. the effect on the child's communication and social functioning in school.

In order to obtain the fullest description possible it is important to take account of the following:

- teacher observation;

- curriculum assessments

- National Curriculum levels;

- behavioural and emotional difficulties, concentration levels and distractibility.

Planning the provision

When planning provision, note particularly any non-verbal strengths which could be utilised. When observations of the child are being made, note:

- 'looking behaviours' which indicate that the child is absorbing information by visual means;

- many children augment their communication with the use of natural gesture and this can provide a useful tool;

- drawing can be useful for a variety of purposes.

2. Curriculum and teaching methods

Consider the following when planning for curriculum teaching:

- Clear marking of the need for attentive listening.

- The interweaving of actions and directions.

- Working specifically on the vocabulary that is required. Do not assume understanding of basic concepts. Be alert to your own use of referential or knowledge terms. Check the child's understanding of key referential terms such as 'middle'.

- Ensuring order-of-mention mirrors order-of-action.

- Using gesture and mime to assist understanding and communication.

- Parallel listening and looking. Demonstrate and show whenever possible. Make expectations clear by showing/modelling behaviour, using drawings, pictures and symbols. Use visual timetables.

- Using pictorial material to assist organisation and as a response from the child, for example in recording.

- Employing mnemonics, for example colour coding and 'idea diagrams' or mind maps.

- Identifying topics of discussion clearly, minimise topic change and signal changes before they happen.

- Making rules and explanations logical, chronologically ordered and explicit.

At School Action Plus and beyond, IEP targets and strategies should include specific language and social communication activities. In addition, approaches such as social skills training, cued articulation or support through a signing system may be found to be useful.

3. Grouping for teaching purposes
- Consider the child's emotional status and the need to be in supportive groups which will enhance and maintain self-esteem.

- Consider grouping carefully when collaborative tasks are being set.

- Map one's ideas about pupil groups on to the various activities that characterise the classroom.

4. Human resources
Teachers and teaching assistants can:

- Work on particular targeted activities suggested by speech and language therapists which require one-to-one work.

- Organise activities such as board games, role play, puppet plays, in which objectives can be pursued in a group, which allows for practice.

- Where children have pragmatic difficulties, support can be utilised to aid the child's understanding of social situations in the classroom and playground and, in the case of older pupils, to analyse where social interactions have broken down.

- Differentially support classroom activities according to where these activities relate to strengths and needs of the child.

Be aware that it is possible for support to be too close. Observation and intervention can be very effective when the child is part of a group in a variety of situations. However, the child can be made to feel different by the constant presence of an adult.

Specialist staff and specific programmes

The speech and language therapist may suggest particular activities, programmes and targets. Bear in mind that:

- These are most effective when incorporated into the curriculum, for example, nominated vocabulary could centre on 'clothes' when such a topic is in progress. Pronouns can be practised in day-to-day classroom interaction.

- Teachers, in company with parents, tend to respond to the meaning of what children say. They therefore feel most at home with the kind of 'correction' that centres on remodelling or expanding children's utterances, for example,

    Child: 'go farm'
    Teacher: 'oh, you went to a farm'

This is an appropriate approach when practising speech and language therapy targets, and is one that is unlikely to undermine frail self-esteem.

- Writing activities provide a legitimate, fruitful and appropriate vehicle for language analysis and teaching. Teacher and child can discuss and problem-solve using a form of language that is 'stable'. Pupils can practise, for example, the use of 'they' instead of repeating the names of characters in a story. For older children this is a particularly useful way of promoting the understanding of how speakers and writers use language to refer back to what has already been said by means of linguistic devices.

Targets for speech intelligibility often require specially constructed and carefully organised activities. It is extremely difficult to provide these in the classroom and in the absence of frequent specialist guidance. They are activities that other children do not require, hence the child cannot be found a group. Individual work is more likely to be indicated in this area and the child may have one-to-one sessions with a speech and language therapist.

At the end of the nominated period, it is very beneficial to discuss specialist learning targets with the speech and language therapist. Some of these targets may have been achieved quickly but some may need breaking down into more manageable steps. Very often, seemingly difficult targets can be remodelled if the therapist is given feedback about the child's response or if details about the learning environment which may limit possibilities are explained.

It is also very important to elicit pupil views and to ensure that the child knows that they are listened to and that their views are valued. This is not always easy to achieve but it can be done by very simple means. For example, a chart on which the skill is recorded and 'happy faces' indicate that the child knows what they are trying to do and how well they have achieved it will serve as a way of drawing them into the activity and helping them to reflect upon their success and enhance their self-esteem.

Classroom activities

In our extract on page 19 the teacher refers to a number of different activities. The following can be identified:

1. Reading

2. Use of apparatus: scissors, glue, paper, materials

3. Writing: sums and writing about clothes

4. Listening: the children are listening

5. Looking: assuming he demonstrated to the red or yellow group

6. Drawing and painting: red group

7. Teacher talking

When Robin Alexander's team examined primary practice, they discovered that taking an activity perspective, rather than a curriculum perspective, gave a sharper impression of what went on in the classroom. They identified a number of 'activities'. The only ones not seen in our example are 'collaboration with other children', although the teacher does mention it to exclude it ('working each on your own', line 27); 'child talking to the class'; and 'construction and movement' which would include PE, games, lining up. Writing was found to be the highest frequency activity (33% of the time) with the other high frequency activities being use of apparatus; reading; listening and looking; drawing and painting. Mathematics was absorbed into writing and use of apparatus. The activity perspective can be useful to identify where children with language difficulties may experience problems and where they may have strengths. Remember that speech and language needs will arise from various types of difficulty and combinations of difficulty and that it is vital to know the child well.

Linking Teaching Objectives with Speech and Language Learning

It may be difficult for the class teacher, with a general view of language as social participation, to work out how general activities lend themselves to teaching objectives that are specifically concerned with speech and language learning. Similarly, a speech and language therapist may not see the opportunities for learning specific speech and language skills in the classroom.

Research carried out by one of the authors shows which activities lend themselves to the focused teaching of particular speech and language skills. The research involved observation of a very experienced teacher in a unit for pupils with speech and language difficulties who at no time had more than eight children to teach. Observation focused on the teacher's language and behaviour when teaching a range of subjects and activities. Even in this setting designed to allow adults to 'work on' children's language, the logic of activities and the social expectations profoundly shaped the speech and language objectives that the teacher could pursue. The main points to emerge were as follows:

1. Opportunities to work with the children on the detail of their speech were rare. Although a teacher could identify a child's error and help them correct it, it would not always be appropriate to do this. In all the activities observed, emphasis on intelligibility would have cut across the learning process. This suggests that intelligibility requires its own specific learning opportunities. An opportunity to work on phonology only occurred when helping the children to spell words in a writing task.

2. An opportunity to help children with grammar only occurred in a writing task. To intervene on grammar in any other observed activity would have been inappropriate.

Taken with Point 1 above, this reinforces the importance of writing as an activity. We have already suggested strategies that link spoken language with literacy (see page 40).

3. The 'number work' task demanded a complete focus on the mathematics involved, with the exception of the precise use of knowledge terms such as 'another', 'middle', 'second'.

4. At all times, it was appropriate to check that the children were paying attention and to clarify that they understood the topic. A wide range of strategies for gaining and maintaining attention and for ensuring that all children were thinking about, referring to, and acting 'to the point', were extensively used.

Working with Parents

The recent revision of the Code of Practice emphasises to an even greater extent the critical role that parents have to play in their children's education. They hold essential information and have unique knowledge and experience to contribute to the shared view of the child's needs and the best ways of supporting them.

The work of teachers and schools can be enhanced considerably when parents are involved in their children's learning and parents can be particularly successful at helping their children at home. They sometimes feel that they need to undertake specific 'programmes' with their children. However, speech and language therapists can provide ideas which can be implemented in natural home settings and it is also helpful for schools to work along these lines in making suggestions which can be incorporated into family life, for example, encouraging the child to make appropriate eye contact or to wait for a turn when speaking. As long as family members do not become too anxious and nag the child, much can be achieved in the informal setting if the child does not feel pressure to perform.

Parents may need help to understand that the best support they can give is to help their child to relax and to provide opportunities to engage in enjoyable family activities. This is particularly so where children are anxious about their difficulties or begin to adopt avoidance behaviours when they recognise speech and language activities.

In the ideal circumstances, schools and parents will work together so that a common or complementary approach can be developed.

Targets to be achieved in a given time should:

- be three or four at most;

- reflect speech and language objectives embedded in the classroom context. So, for example, the target for an older pupil might be 'to help the listener to understand what s/he is talking about', by marking topics;

- reflect specialist suggestions woven into the context of the curriculum;

- be achievable while extending skill;

- reflect stages leading to more substantial targets where appropriate, for example to practise saying a particular sound at the ends of words, rather than an expectation that it will be pronounced appropriately in all positions in words;

- be understood by all involved. Issues of speech and language are complex. Ensure that everyone who is working with the child has some understanding and realistic expectations concerning targets;

- be recorded;

- be reviewed with an explicit timetable.

Pastoral Care

There are specific issues relevant for the child with speech and language difficulties with a need to ensure that all members of staff who come into contact with the pupil understand the particular difficulties. For example, dinner supervisors might find it helpful to know that a child has problems with understanding language or has word-finding difficulties which might interfere with the ability to answer questions or to make choices in a busy situation. Speech and language difficulties may create many obstacles to getting through the school day and it can be helpful to anticipate some of the pitfalls.

Parents may wish to discuss matters of concern. It is not uncommon for children with language and communication difficulties to behave in more challenging ways at home than they do at school. The school may be the first point of contact for parents' anxieties and it is important to be responsive to their concerns. It can be useful to be familiar with local support systems and networks which parents can access.

Even where there are no behavioural problems, parents may feel that they are in some way to blame for their child's difficulties. They may question what they might or might not have done to precipitate them. Schools need to be sensitive, positive and reassuring in their relationships with parents. Speech and language therapists may be of assistance in this respect, helping parents and teachers to understand the nature and origins of speech and language needs.

In Conclusion

The identification of key teaching and learning objectives for a child depends on an assessment of both the child and the classroom, including the adults who plan and organise the learning environment. The aim is to assist the child in becoming an effective communicator and to use language and communication skills for the range of learning activities in school. At the beginning of this book, we noted that language and communication needs are addressed within the child's social and educational environment. The activities outlined above take account of language difficulties within the demands of the curriculum and the organisation of classroom tasks. Activities that use and promote language for the child with special needs as part of daily classroom routines also benefit other pupils. Modification of the classroom environment, effected by changing teachers' own language, is an important strategy for engaging children in learning. The focus therefore is not only the language of the children but also the communication skills of the adults.

Effective communication is also the key to collaboration between practitioners engaged with the child, and their family members. Language learning is never complete. We hope that this book will promote more discussion of language and communication needs and will lead the way to more effective practice.

References

Alexander, R. (1995) *Versions of primary education.* London: Routledge.

Bloom, L. and Lahey, M. (1978) *Language development and language disorders.* New York: Wiley.

Boehm, R. (1986) *Boehm test of basic concepts.* London: The Psychological Corporation, Harcourt, Brace and Company.

Conti-Ramsden, G. and Botting, N. (1999) 'Classification of children attending language units in England: a national study of 7 year olds'. *International Journal of Language and Communication Disorders.* 34, 359–66.

Department for Education and Employment and Qualifications and Curriculum Authority (1999) *The National Curriculum: Handbook for teachers in England Key Stages 1 and 2.* London: DfEE and QCA.

Department for Education and Skills (2001) *Special Educational Needs Code of Practice.* London: Department for Education and Skills.

Dewart, H. and Summers, S. (1995) *Pragmatics Profile of Everyday Communication Skills in Children.* Windsor: NFER-Nelson.

Lacey, P. (2001) *Support Partnerships: collaboration in action.* London: David Fulton.

Locke, A. and Beech, M. (1991) *Teaching Talking.* Windsor: NFER-Nelson.

Oxford Reading Tree (1986) Oxford: Oxford University Press.

Ripley, K., Barrett, J. and Fleming, P. (2001) *Inclusion for Children with Speech and Language Impairments.* London: David Fulton.

Wright, J. (1996) 'Teachers and therapists: the evolution of a partnership'. *Child Language Teaching and Therapy.* 12, 1, 3–14.

Further Reading

Harris, J. (1990) *Early language development: implications for clinical and educational practice.* London: Routledge.

Law, J. and Elias, J. (1996) *Trouble Talking.* London: Jessica Kingsley.

Martin, D. and Miller, C. (2003) *Speech and language difficulties in the classroom,* 2nd Edition. London: David Fulton.

Resources

Child Language Teaching and Therapy. Published by Arnold, London. This journal publishes reports of research and practice in the field of speech and language difficulties. It is available at special rates to members of NAPLIC (see below).

Starting Points: a resource pack on speech and language difficulties: Available from West Sussex County Council Education Department.

Useful Addresses

AFASIC
50–52 Great Sutton Street
London EC1V ODJ
Tel: 020 74909410
www.afasic.org.uk

Glossary sheets and other information are available from AFASIC on many aspects of speech and language difficulty.

ICAN
4 Dyars Buildings
Holborn
London EC1Y 9NH

A voluntary body for children with special needs. Has publications and information on many aspects of communication disability.

National Association of Professionals concerned with Language
Impairment in Children (NAPLIC)
Contact through: naplicnewsletter@btinternet.com

A multidisciplinary organisation for practitioners in speech and language
difficulties. Holds an annual conference and provides information on
aspects of speech and language.

Royal College of Speech and Language Therapists
2 White Hart Yard
London
SE1 1NX
Tel: 020 7378 1200
http://www.rcslt.org

The professional body for speech and language therapists. Publishes
Communicating Quality, the professional standards for speech and language
therapists working in different settings, including education.

Observation Guide

Below we have attempted to establish a guide to the classroom observation of a child with suspected or known speech and language difficulties. We have identified questions to ask as a way of pointing to key aspects of the situations being observed. You may wish to develop the guide into a schedule or record form with space after each question for your comments. It may be helpful to use a tape recorder for some of the activities.

Activities

1. Which activities did the child engage in during your observation period(s)?

   Examples: writing, use of apparatus, movement, drawing and painting, construction, reading, listening and looking, collaborative, talk to class, talk with teacher.

The teacher's behaviour when giving information and instructions

2. Did the teacher alert the student to listen? For example, say their name or ask the child to look at them? Did they ask for the attention of the child's group?

3. Were instructions given in a way that matched the sequence of stages in the activity?

4. How many separate parts were there to the instruction? For example, there are three in 'go to your drawer and get it (library book) and go to the library.'

5. Which referential (knowledge) terms were used? For example, through, first, few, around, middle.

6. Were key words identified for the students?

7. In what form was the information presented? Verbal: prose, rhyme, story, song. Non-verbal: symbol (including writing), image, scene, diagram, model.

8. Did the teacher use sign, gestures or mime?

9. Was the child shown how to do the task?

10. Was the child shown a finished example?

The child's overall behaviour in response to the teacher
11. Did the child succeed in carrying out the task as requested?

12. Did the child 'disobey' or fail to carry out instructions?

13. Did the child start the activity late and begin by looking at what the other children were doing?

14. Did the child fall out with the other children involved?

15. Did the child spontaneously comment on what they were doing?

16. Did the child make any spontaneous general remarks unrelated to the activity?

17. Did the child seek assistance either verbally or non-verbally?

18. Did the child show evidence of grasping the topic?

19. Did the child show evidence of grasping the point of the activity?

The teacher's overall behaviour in response to the child
20. Does the teacher give adequate time for the child to verbally respond?

21. Does the teacher encourage other children to give adequate time for the child to speak?

22. Does the teacher encourage the child to show what they understand, and how?

For example, by speaking, writing, key word diagram, scene drawing, cartoon drawing, gesture and mime, through computer facilitation, model, map.

The child's spoken language during activities
23. Does the child produce all sounds accurately?

24. Is the length of the child's sentences age-appropriate?

25. Is the order of the words correct?

26. Does the child select appropriate words?

27. Does the child speak fluently, without difficulty in finding words?

28. How do you rate the child's overall intelligibility?

The child's other responses to tasks
29. How do you rate the child's drawing ability?

30. How do you rate the child's organisational ability?

31. How do you rate the child's motor skills?

The child's behaviour when in collaboration with other children
32. Does the child grasp conversational topics and changes of topic?

33. Does the child grasp the point of the activity and changes in the direction of the activity?

34. Does the child take turns in conversation?

35. Does the child get attention in conversation?

36. Does the child give attention in conversation?

37. Does the child repair conversations?

38. Does the child speak in relation to the activity?

39. Does the child take turns in the activity?

40. Does the child get attention in the activity?

41. Does the child give attention in the activity?

42. Does the child repair activities, for example, get the scissors just when they are needed?

43. Does the child contribute to somebody else's activity, for example, suggest something or give a piece of equipment or material?

44. Does the child incorporate someone else's suggestion or material?

The child's behaviour when writing
45. Is the child's choice of ideas adequate?

46. Is the ordering of ideas adequate?

47. Is the sentence structure correct?

48. Is the choice of words appropriate?

49. Does the child find words readily?

50. Is the child's spelling correct? (Note errors.)

51. Does the child write easily, legibly and with appropriate sizing?

52. Can the child read back their own writing?

53. Does the child read back over what they have written so far as a way of successfully completing a sentence or a story?

The child's behaviour when reading
54. Is the child's recognition of words age-appropriate?

55. Do they recognise words easily or is it a slow process?

56. Does the child show a mastery of word attack? (Syllables, onset and rime and letter sounds.)

57. Does the child comprehend the individual word meanings?

58. Does the child comprehend the sentence structure?

59. Does the child comprehend the topic?

General
60. Is the child happy and relaxed?

Appendix 2
A Glossary of some Terms used in this book

Articulators Any specific part of the vocal apparatus involved in the production of sound.

Content The topic and ideas encoded in messages.

Discourse A continuous stretch of language (especially spoken).

Fluency Smoothness with which sounds, syllables, words and phrases are joined together during oral language.

Form The phonological, morphological or syntactic characteristics of the language. The means for connecting sound with meaning.

Grammar The structural organisation of a language.

Intonation The distinctive use of patterns of pitch or melody.

Language An organised set of symbols used for communication.

Levels of language A general term used in linguistics to refer to a major dimension of structural organisation held to be susceptible to independent study.

Morpheme The minimal distinctive unit of grammar.

Morphology The study of the structure or forms of words.

Object A term used in the analysis of grammatical functions to refer to a major constituent of sentence or clause structure, traditionally associated with the 'receiver' or 'goal' of an action.

Onset The initial consonant(s) of a word.

Phonetics	The science that studies the characteristics of human sound-making.
Phonology	The study of the sound systems of languages.
Pitch	The attribute of auditory sensation in terms of which a sound may be ordered on a scale from 'low' to 'high'.
Pragmatics	The aspect of meaning that is concerned with the relationship between the utterances of speakers and the contexts in which they are spoken.
Received Pronunciation (RP)	Considered to be speech without an obvious regional accent.
Referent	The object, situation, action to which a linguistic expression refers.
Rime	The vowel and final consonant(s) of a word.
Semantics	The meaning of words in utterances.
Speech	The spoken medium for the transmission of language.
Standard English	Broadly, the form of English normally used in writing, on radio and television and the dialect of English normally taught to foreign learners.
Stress	The degree of force used in producing a syllable.
Subject	A term used in the analysis of grammatical functions to refer to a major constituent of sentence or clause structure, traditionally associated with the 'doer' of an action.
Syllable	A unit of pronunciation typically larger than a single sound and smaller than a word. According to most authorities, the syllable is easy to identify but difficult to define.

Syntax	Traditional term for the study of the rules governing the way in which words are combined to form sentences in a language.
Transcription	A written record of speech.
Use	The function of language; the reasons why people speak and choose alternative forms for different purposes.
Utterance	A sequence of words produced by a speaker in a specific context.
Voice quality	Term used in phonetics to refer to the permanently present, background, person-identifying feature of speech.

AFASIC

overcoming speech impairments

AFASIC represents children and young people who are unable to communicate effectively because of speech and language impairments. Our mission is to promote understanding, acceptance, equal opportunities and the integration into society of those we represent. Those at the heart of our work have difficulties that are not the result of another physical or intellectual disability and can be seen as on the continuum from autism to dyslexia.

AFASIC's work involves:

- providing information and organising conferences, seminars for parents and professionals on speech and language impairments;

- providing direct support for young people by organising Activity Weeks and Social Skills Courses, both of which include challenging new activities to develop self-esteem and social skills;

- working alongside other organisations who share AFASIC's interest in the field of education, health, training and employment;

- liaising with central and local government in order to improve existing services and available support.